rock painter
poems by R.E. Rashley

TURNSTONE PRESS

Acknowledgements:

R.E. Rashley's poems have appeared — or will appear — in the following magazines, journals and anthologies: *Arbos, Arts Manitoba, The Canadian Forum, Contemporary Verse/Two, Essays in Canadian Writing, Grain, Horizon: Writings of The Canadian Prairie, Number One Northern, Saskatchewan Harvest, Skylark, The Artist in Canadian Literature* and *The English Quarterly.*

He published four books of poetry, including *Voyageur and Other Poems, Portrait and Other Poems* and *Moon Lake and Other Poems,* all in the Ryerson Chapbook series, and *Paso Por Aqui* with Fiddlehead Press in 1973.

Mr. Rashley also published numerous articles, reviews and a critical book entitled *Poetry in Canada: The First Three Steps* (Ryerson: 1958). This latter book is being reprinted by Tecumseh Press in Ottawa.

ISBN 0-88801-014-1 hard cover
0-88801-013-3 soft cover

Copyright © 1978, the estate of R.E. Rashley
Introduction Copyright, Terrence Heath

CONTENTS

- 8 Introduction
- 11 Semaphore
- 12 Rock Painter
- 13 At Grey Owl's Cabin
- 14 Hanson Lake Road
- 15 Paso por aqui
- 16 Magpie
- 17 Bull-roarer
- 18 Wilderness
- 19 Martin's Lake
- 20 At Pelican Narrows
- 21 What lies under the prairie
- 22 Make like a poet
- 23 Portrait of an Indian
- 24 For C.L.H.
- 26 Homestead revisited: for M.E.R.
- 27 Night journey and departure
  - Meeting at night
- 29   Airport
- 30   People
- 31 Homecoming
- 32 Admonition to Germaine
- 33 Slides
- 34 Love poem
- 35 Against togetherness
- 36 Marianne
- 37 Incident at Adamson Lake
- 38 Showing slides
- 39 Things to know
- 40 Cool
- 41 Error
- 42 Autumn reflection
- 43 Children's exhibition
- 44 Chokecherry pits
- 45 Chinese food for the party
- 46 Gleanings
- 47 Dock Street
- 48 Lost reply
- 49 From a time of drought
  - Renewal
- 50   After the dust storm
- 51   Love among the ruins
- 52 Hollow in the wheat and blackbirds
- 53 On the river
- 54 Song, returning
- 55 Caterpillar
- 56 Waste
- 57 Endpiece: Burning the leaves

Introduction

    In the last days of November, 1975, I opened the manuscript for the book of poems by R.E. Rashley which you are holding. The strong smell of cigarette smoke rose from the pages and, although he had died more than two weeks before, he sat across from me again, smoking his interminable cigarettes, his eyes half-hooded by his lids, his quiet voice hardly moving his lips as it passed out of his body. And, again, he was talking about my poetry, giving me in bits and pieces his aesthetic: poetry is lean and disciplined; it is common; it is exact; it reverbrates its own sounds, but never indulges itself; it is personal, but reaches for the universal; it has its own shape which it will find for itself; it is worked up; it is best ironic and understated; it does not seek its audience, it creates it; it is final when printed.

    R.E. Rashley was a very important poet. If he is considered minor, it is only because he wrote so little and has been so little published. To those of us who were admitted to the wealth that lay behind his few poems, he gave a "voice" which came from the experience of this prairie place. Long before regionalism and the recent cultural nationalism, he affirmed that he was an artist living here at this time and wrote out of all he saw and knew and sensed. He seems to me the quintessential prairie writer. His poetry was not written for acceptance by eastern literary magazines or Toronto audiences. It was not written for any audience. He wrote with a pure desire to speak, not with a desire to be heard.

    Besides his own poetry, which he only showed me after I had known him many years, he offered a thorough knowledge of Canadian poetry. And, he was a bibliophile who owned a collection of Canadian poetry and writing probably unrivalled in this part of the country. But he didn't talk about poetry in general. He believed that only the individual poem mattered. He eschewed talk about biography, origins, influences and the other well-worn aberrations of the critical intellect. He wanted all his life to create his own poems and to re-create the poems of others.

Two nights before his death, I sat with him and went through each of the poems in this book. We had always talked about my poetry; now, he wanted me to talk about his. Every poem was scrutinized: Do you like this one? Does it work? Why doesn't it? Where? How? I felt my enormous ignorance and lack of seriousness in the face of this man's lonely passion for the word. He didn't notice my uneasiness, my hesitancies; he heard only my opinions and strained to bridge the gap between my understanding of his poems and his act of making the poems. He struck me later as almost desperate.

As I left, he turned to me and said, "You know, I've never known a writer before." Even as I write down his comment, it produces in me the same sense of terror and pride that it did that evening.

Then, he was dead, and I sat in chapel listening to his close friend, George Dyck, reading one of his poems, "Moonlake" (which is not included in this collection). I realized how irretrievably gone he was; he consumed all things he encountered in life, and when he was consumed, there was nothing left, except these poems which are his life:

> this aromatic smoke lifting,
> voices of children fat with pleasure tasted,
> thin grey ash.

— Terrence Heath

Semaphore

The sun blinks
at the astonished afternoon
as a hill sprouts flags staccato.
There, in the distance,
suddenly flags snap back.

Do not complain
the semaphore
does violence to your sense of wilderness.
Boys are irreverent;
they will squirt the sun's eye, even,
at clouds, with mirrors,
and call their impudence heliograph.
Read it another way,
it is heroic
to tickle space
with the bright flicker.
The impish is not out of context here,
nor the gnomic.
Unreal signals coming from real places
mock our readings;
real encounters trouble our looking-glass lands.

And I,
having failed to understand
the little shadow that crossed your face
unheralded, yesterday,
have to assume things such as flags
or sun flashes
are adequate enough
communication.

Rock painter

The man stood in a canoe
(and a neat trick
since any pressure would float it away)
and I wonder,
standing uneasily, too,
did he know it before he came to the place
hurrying to say it while it was there to say
or did he search for it patiently
finding it by degrees in the rock face?
Irrelevant questions.
Whether I came or not
was nothing to him.
It is not an eloquent thought
inviting discussion —
a private performance
functioning privately.
He kneaded his handful of coloured muck
and structured himself on rock
building a platform
to play his life tolerably.

At Grey Owl's cabin

The man with the dyed hair
playing at Indian
no longer talks
to the wild things.

Whether he was or was not
playing a part
would not have mattered to them —
he was real in their cabin
whatever had happened before.

At least, one may say,
playing one's own life as one can,
it is evident something good
has gone from the place —

no loon has cried from the lake all day
the beaver do not come here any more.

Hanson Lake Road

Immense pavement after a rain,
every unevenness full of the glass-pure water.
Quiet, heavy enough to breathe,
to float in —

A frantic lynx trying to get four kittens
over the road-way,
an agony of anxiety restless
in the low bushes —

Indian children at Pelican Narrows
friendly and photogenic
laughing pictures wanting to be taken —

Picnic lakes
gilded fish hanging at ease
in the sun-bright shallows —

And new experience of you,
relaxed, smiling under the pines,
hands filled with cones.
You!
Good traveller!

Paso por aqui

Somewhere along this ridge the man who struck
became the stricken,
whatever he meant to be
razed to a cryptic message,
a little debris.
No cry came out of the spaces then,
and now no cry —
The almost speaking
is just the windy places
shifting still.

I only see
an almost hopeless exercise in recovery,
bone,
stone,
ash,
glacial till.

Magpie

I see you
pecking creatures
spattered on hardtop
in the night.

I call you
scavenger.

You reply
with that beautiful
straight-line flight.

Bull-roarer

It is not the magnificent we are concerned with here,
not even the useful —
the point that struck bone and was broken
the pot ill-tended that burned in the fire
awls
scrapers
beads
shards
discards;

not a great people tearing monoliths
out of the living rock,
thrusting up spires,
crusading;
people mating, grubbing out roots, shaping,
squatting by fires.

But the wet clay patterned with rabbit-skin cords
one understands;
it could hardly be thought to aspire
but there is a sort of meeting of hands —

and my little son,
exploring the field,
has threaded the bone disc through its holes
on a piece of string.
Whirling it round his head
he stirs his blood
with the fine roaring.

Wilderness

The rock was adamant.
It could not enter me.
Around it stood
a stonehenge circle of great trees.
I was the pupil of an eye
staring at nothing
and through that pupil
the wilderness drained me.

I wished for something to descend
that could secure me.

Came
a raven
on tilted wings.
The rock uncovered a glittering eye
that stared at me.

And I stared out through the circle of trees
and the rock stared into me.

Martin's Lake

At Martin's Lake the clouds descended
and struck us with ice.
There was nothing alive in that air,
nothing but us contained in the car
and hail that rattled and bounced on metal
slipping into the water.

After,
the sun caught shallows with light
between the lake ice and the shore.
We stood and watched
a fish
like a little shadow —

and for this place
this was life —
a four-inch creature
hung
between ice
and rock that seemed colder
than ice.

At Pelican Narrows

The children
splashing and shouting
an hour ago
are gone.
The froth of laughter has settled into the lake.

I am going, myself.
I can not do what I want to do,
with my equipment,
cramped, alone,
knees wedging ridges harder than bone.
My lens will not make the rock-struck flower
richer, more credible, visible even.

I slip the camera cover on
and flex my knees against the ache.

Slowly, coldly, on the lake,
a loon's cry
wells into emptiness
of laughter being gone.

What lies under the prairie

Lost stones
brown translucent slaying stones
game stones
trade stones
medicine stones (failed stones)
fire baked, made stones
used stones
touched stones
crumbling stones that lie around old hearths
where women worked

(hair streaming forward black from bent heads
breasts swaying)

lost, lost
lost

Make like a poet

One need not always make like a poet
to make poetry.
Major things happen off-stage —
a telegram's tilted words
sorted out privately.

One may stride into the square
whirling a severed head
spattering brains and blood
to clear a space effectively.

There are other suitable places
one may inhabit
quietly.

Portrait of an Indian

Spring made little promise
and the summer burned.
Fall came meagrely.
Winter struck with a blade of ice.
The years, one after the other, were much in this wise.

And one spoke, in defeat, counselling his people:
"From nothing we come, into nothing we go.
A little shadow runs across the grass
into the sunset".

One warrior was covered with wounds.
He delighted in saying
how he had broken the feathered ends
and thrust the bared rods out through his body.
Indeed, it was true;
it could have been done in no other way.

Only those survived
who grew to unrelenting vigilance,
who lit their counter-fires of patience
down wind against the blaze
and thrust against the ice, as cold, as hard,
pride.

A bitter clime!
But where else, out of only flesh and bone,
could time carve out such perverse granite
or wind and winter mate like this in line.

For C.L.H.

A sprinkle of rain
litters the grass with crocus
and the afternoon
murmurs with growing.
The river again slips quietly under its bridges
multiplying the city.

Even the night is lovely, trafficked with lights
like drops of blood trickling over the bridge,
hanging for seconds, giving and flowing.
The signals pump and the city moves and is living,
making its face up, now, for April,
careless of old lovers,
unremembering.

The drops of blood quiver across the water
where the river unreluctant to its mouth
pours out its tawny flood
as it did, long, long ago
while the nomads paused there
to bury a woman, with her jewels, her dignity,
suddenly seeing nothing.

It is not the dead who remember,
standing by raw earth in the falling snow
or in rain under the dripping trees —
and the people who gathered there on the plains
high over the river to inter —
were they making a solemn ritual for her
who was gone, or for them who remained?
What is violated is not the woman lovingly placed
but the living who thought

man was more than a coyote running over the waste;

and the circumstance is of little weight —
the slow change of a dying season,
the shock that dropped a city below its harbour,
the breaking of a vessel in the brain
simply equate
to the tongues that came whispering into my tree
and hung speaking
and are silent of late.

And the bright season,
walking with Spring along the river,
does not quite charm us to forget.
The mirroring stream does not turn back.
April is tainted already with September.

Whether the river we live by is tawny
or crimson
it will do as well as the black.

Homestead revisited: for M.E.R.

It is all so very small —
Where the wide doors, the high wall?

The room that was the very center —
one wanders helplessly about.
One has entered so many times before,
why is it one can no longer enter?

It is hopeless to say, "At last we are home".
This is not the place.
Let us go.
It was a mistake to come.

Night journey and departure

1. Meeting at night

One remembers the road flowing from moulded corners
slowly emerging into runnels of sound.
One remembers the sense slowly converging,
folding its frayed antennae
into the soothing texture,
being nothing,
flowing along a tube into the night.

One remembers the eyes
flaring along the shadowed way,
unseen creatures of the wood
turning to stare
their intense baleful stare.

The shock of storm
crashing into attention,
wipers beating their fragile hands into the flood,
the rocking car,
the crawling —

The highway patrolman further along the route,
time running out with the dome light
churning its pulse of blood.
Impossible questions —
searching for symbols in the glove compartment,
holding up charts,
proofs —
Somehow one made responses,
spoke the expected words —

The road, again, pulling under and under
down the darkened chute.

One remembers
the town, the hotel, the night clerk emerging,
personal, speaking official words —
greeting.

The long drive home,
the talk,
the night air sweet in the side windows,
the stop to stretch legs at the roadside tables,
treading the earth,
the dark flowers of the leaves —

It was good, then, to be going,
and, if one could, one would gladly do it again,
but such things are a flowing.
Now it is all pulled under
what one remembers most is the earth smell
and the dark flowers of the leaves.

2. Airport

The tantalizing, false, blue lights
blink as the great beast crosses
and, tamely, at heel, rolls in.
Things eaten at Edmonton
or further west disgorge.
It is time to part,
time for the words that cover, not conceal,
carefully tying
nothings to inane nothings,
lying —

A sudden bell shatters the quiet,
looses a clatter of indirections into the night
as if someone with a bright insensate laugh
lifted the top of the head and dropped in a handful of glass.

And the plane tears at the clutching grass
violent to be alone.
It is all right,
as the great thing grows toward flight,
to be saying with the mind,
"They are all gone into that world of light",
but the blood is crying plainly enough,
"The world is night".

3. People

Some are sharp circles
carelessly looped over the creeping world,
hawks.

Some, sleek,
neat little black and white penguins
poised on precarious ice.

One, I saw, once,
flash vivid and scarlet,
lifting obscurity into green light.

Some never soar
but hop with careful feet
curled to the branch of their security.
Safe wingless birds,
dead to delight!

There is some danger in flight.

Homecoming

Me! peering out
between legs like trunks of trees
at shadows,
warming at spurts of laughter,
whittling my own things
from discarded things they made —

Me! climbing trunks
to hear what the wind says —

Me!

Voices on voices people
the still grove
rooted in me,
still shedding leaves
and shade.

Admonition to Germaine

How lovely, your room, overlooking the river,
after the indignity of probe and knife,
and the fall has never been so rich.
The children have been taking pictures
all afternoon in the bright sun,
staying the sweet, decaying season.

I have been with them, but alone,
idly dutiful,
touching the garments thrown in lovely profusion,
stirring with patient feet dry leaves
that rustle and break
like brittle blood.

Ah, Love! returning from such cold embrace,
look forward steadily, do not look back.
The season is only enchanted — a lip's touch,
it will recover and never miss
the rain of riches.
It is not so with us —
just one poor loveliness is all we have to clutch.

Slides

The ornate structures assemble in instant light
roads over mountain passes
silent crowds
and the coloured signs that no one can understand
and we finally come to the end
and the last sherry

and everyone says that was great
a real tour
a person has to be better for seeing
all those beautiful things
say, how could they move all those stones?

And we untangle
skillfully
calling goodbyes all the way out to the car

and on the way home you say
I would have liked some prairie
and later
after the ripples have rippled out to the edge
of my mind
I think
You're in luck
that's all you can get from me.

Love poem

The boy and girl walking
the river road, stepping
together —
I feel like saying to them,
"Where the road bends
a little path
runs up into the hills.
Under a maple there the earth is warm
and sweet with old loving".

Inside, the house is golden light.
Here, the snow flakes drop to your cheek,
touch, melt
before I can touch them.
No footprints lead toward you;
none away.

Droplets of green and gold
trickle over the hill —
scouts homing.
Suddenly you are gone
to your sons' coming.

One sparrow teeters in the wind
with tipped-up feathers.
Bright as sunlight
on the patio the flock
gather your bread crumbs.

For many years now we have gathered
bitter fruit,
mouth-puckering chokecherries,
which somehow transmute
into crimson wine
rich syrup.

So here am I
after all these years
learning to write
a love poem.

Against togetherness

I do not seek company as a rule
nor entertain.

My wine is chokecherry,
bitter for cultured tastes.
I dine on goldeye,
grouse,
deer.

I do not import
what pleases another one.

It is not that cities are out of reach
but uglier
than these places.
Trees distort
trying for not enough sun.

Marianne

When I think of Marianne
I always remember the bird in the cage.

As one talked to her
she would frequently turn
to make little whispering whistles with parted lips.
She would smooth the flowered plumage with gentle
            fingers.
Sometimes she would open the cage
and tempt the bird to flutter a little in the air
half delighting in flight
half trembling at freedom.
"Be sure the windows are closed", she would say.
"Can you see the neighbour's cat?"

It was difficult enough without the bird,
difficult to conform,
with those parted lips and caressing gestures,
that capacity for caring —
"Marianne", one might imagine oneself to say,
"Marianne" — beginning —
but there was the bird fluttering
and Marianne turned away.

One ended by wondering what it really was
on delicate feathers fluttering,
what, in the woman, the bird had become,
too difficult to touch,
reaching, however gently, through filigree and fluff.

Incident at Adamson Lake

walking the ancient beach
simply looking at grass, trees, flowers

returning at last to the car
and the lunch
and hearing the strange small roar
of spruce, in one place only, threshing
on the far shore
in one place
everywhere else as quiet as before —
a dust devil (only there's no dust here)
moving out to the water
sucking a circle of waves into a white squall.
If it had been less local
we probably would have ducked into the car
but — one spot in the lake boiling?
we sat watching it come
and suddenly it was there
skirt, shirt whipping
garbage can lids, picnic basket, things from the table
leaping into the air —

and, after
breathlessly
running through slough grass
picking up knives, forks, cups
and the basket lodged in trees

and, before we left,
the highway patrolman,
making his routine call,
suspicious, eyeing us,
disbelief in his face
"Say, what went on here, anyway?
What happened in this place?"

and home in the late day
pushing out windows
giving ourselves to the night air
and to bed
and the whirled together embrace
and no policeman this time
breaking the spent quiet
"Hey, what happened in this place?"

37

Showing slides

Campsite —
We took it because of the lilies.
                The stench
                that goes with the water
                doesn't come through,
                nor the glittering raven black as
                          fractured coal
                tearing at garbage.

Lunch by Lake Shawnoe.
                This was surprise,
                the incredible rightness
                of picnics up on the bulge of the world —
                not the irrelevant rock,
                but the loons crying the same cry
                one to the other,
                each hearing the same cry.

A rocky point taken to keep
the feel of the place.
                It does not put your foot in the sponge
                of needles rotting —
                You bury fingers,
                tempted to take off shoes,
                wanting to take some home
                for winter flowers
                red as the woodpecker's crest
                that rattled a message in code.

Carla, sunset, under the trees.
                — coded rich
                like the rotting tree.
                The glittering raven coded,
                the golden tree —
                the crimson glittering tree —
                sweet, grovelling, bitter ecstacy —

She looks nice.
                She looks *nice*?
                You think she looks NICE?
                N I C E ?

                Christ!

No more slides to see.

Things to know

The clutched flowers had no names —
just common ones
like roses —
you gave up asking anyone,
nobody knew.
You made your peace with the thing itself —
red, sweet, pricky —
as it came to you.

There's no use asking the kids
to make it
on names you needed
that long ago.

Funny!
It doesn't matter!

They push out an asphalt playground
over the yellow violets

and asphalt they know.

Cool

Came down sweat-soaked
and breathy
to a pool

slowly
pulling the great still trees
myself lilies branches birds floating in these
together
eyeing illusion
flowers
rooted in wavering flowers
bird plunging its beak
into its own beak

envying fish
firm and free in the true element
breathing it in and out —
smooth —
green stone cool

Error

Nature is always right
I thought
especially birds
mirrored on water
perfectly
cleaving the air

and the duck launched
from a spatter of foam
across my car

I, unconcerned,
reading the wings
waiting to share
the last eloquent lift

which did not occur

Autumn reflection

From spring through summer as I planned
the border answered to my hand.

The quiet carpeting of grass
defended where the crowds pass.

Flowers stood richly to the eye
and people smiled as they passed by.

Occurrences quite unforeseen,
of late, disturb the garden scene.

These leaves I did not plan at all
I gather them because they fall.

Children's exhibition

The lines suggest
but do not quite detach
the figure from the street —
part of the buildings, just discernible,
one eye a window, brick, is it wall or cheek?
part of the texture, even.

What does the child see, then?
Doesn't she know
a man is more than anything that he makes?
or, at least, I always thought so.

Yet here she arranges trifles a bird might snatch,
fragments of meanings picked into nothing
unconcernedly.

I see myself in the eye of a bird —
of no identity.

Chokecherry Pits

The contour lines follow the old humus.
Trowel and brush work easily down
through the shallow droppings of time.
Stone grates — maybe a flake —
or is it a tool emerging?
"How can you tell!", people wonder.
Tools fit themselves into the function.
Hands and fingers, it seems, were always the same.
The brush comes out, and, suddenly, "Hey! Beads!" —
little black spheres in the ashes —
They are not beads, we discover —
chokecherry pits,
tossed or spat into the fire.

It was August, then, when this hearth was burning!
I picture chokecherries spread in the sun,
lustrous, crimson — rolled, and shifted, and sampled —
pemmican.
Suddenly I remember
pulling the branches down for someone,
watching the drops of blood
trickle through curled fingers —
With us it was jelly or wine.

I kneel for a moment, cupping the charred pits,
by a rekindled hearth,
a patch of chickweed spread like a white table,
wine, pemmican,
prairie sun,
wind sliding over the great erosion,
old brown river cutting a way to the sea.

Chinese food for the party,

oriental decor
old friends
familiar as wolf willow
saying "Delicious!"

into the talk and laughter
teasing memory
sweet as the western flower
slips an intruder —

coming from furlough
trains running late
missing connections
waiting, waiting,
waiting —
at Tormentine
getting so hungry I took the cake
intended for friends
and the wharf was so cold
I finally got to the wine.

Food for a king!
Flavour of home!

but who was ever a king
licking a bottle neck
alone

Gleanings

The nature club is having a field day
in the bright autumn.
We pass them here and there on our route
to an ancient site,
made happier by their abandonment to delight.

They are gathering still
when we turn for home.
A woman is standing at rendezvous,
a gorgeous cluster of crimson leaves
springing up from her hand over her breast.
Should we stop and help her identify
Rhus radicans Rudbergii —
poison ivy?
No. She would only turn away.
We are dirty after a day of digging —
in old clothes.
Who wants rejection from loveliness?
Or, for that matter, who wants to be told
what loveliness is,
waiting, unaware —

We pass along,
our gatherings safely stored in the trunk,
and leave her standing there.

Dock Street

Three girls go by in civvies, walking,
legs in silk stockings, thighs under gay skirts,
brightly talking.
The wind picks up the playing muscles;
the perfume hangs for a moment richly;
the eyes blur —

The tip of his wife's ear, delicate, scented!

The lonely wind bickers along the store-fronts
pries at the guttered leaves
picks at the sleeves with cold unfriendly fingers.

Buy a paper, Mister, buy a poppy,
buy a *Liberty*, buy a ticket for the bazaar,
Gimme a nickel, Mister, gimme a cent,
Buy a ticket, gimme a nickel —

Ask him to buy a ticket back west!

Bitterly the grey bay creeps in on its shore-line;
salt wind blows from the dead water;
strange sea-fowl lift harsh discordant laughter.

Lost reply

In spring a mallard
sudden in the weed-edge.

Then broken shell
and replicas
skittering into the reeds,
the slough alive with splashing.

Yesterday, silence.

Now the minute wedges
high, high,
and the heart-tearing cry.

Something responds.
Some shadowy inner thing
goes echoing.

And I will not go to the slough tomorrow
to stand face turned to the sky.

From a time of drought

1. Renewal

   The seasons alter, renewing the purple crocus,
   flaming the tiger lily out of the parched sod.

   The sinews pull, the lean muscle tenses,
   the bar moves drily on its fulcrum
   and the voyageur bears into the season.

   In winter's ice and summer's furnace tested,
   brazed by the snow that shifts and the sand that sifts,
   tissues tanned and roughened and sanded down,
   time hardened and usage worn, substance gaunted,
   the voyageur bears into the picking wind
   unrested.

   The seasons alter, restoring the purple crocus,
   tossing the wild rose to riot along the fences,
   flaming their multicolours over the late skies.
   The voyageur lifts darkly in the crucible of sunset
   his weary silhouette, irreducible and unrefined,
   black in the bright focus.

2. After the dust storm

> The furrow lines are bossed with rippled drifts,
> the drill half-buried, but the drilled seed lost,
> each stone, each bone,
> on its sculptured cliff, lifts, wind erected,
> living and dead rejected.
>
> Elsewhere forgotten men lie back in deep caverns.
> Here, where the wind over all things sifts
> dry desolation,
> out of the razed earth, grinning, the voyageur
> comes, naked, cameoed,
> raised for the wind to pick at, the dust to abrade.
>
> O rootless race!
> lay not your bones here in the quick soil
> lest unhappily they toil
> back to the wind's frustration,
> the sun's desiccation.

3. Love among the ruins

　　Chores done, close in the windbreak's corner,
　　Tom and the hired girl sit and look at the future,
　　night closing in and the strong wind wearying.

　　"Another few years, this will be mine to share.
　　Take it, be mistress. Next year the field, God willing,
　　will yield for us, rain fulfilling,
　　rich will the harvest be. Take it, be wife of it all."

　　She nothing answers, crisping the grass in her fingers,
　　feeling the sand drift its film on her cheek,
　　and hearing the dry grasshoppers brittle creak.

　　"A builder my father was; he built this house.
　　Paint it, next year it will be good as new.
　　Fill it with all you desire to comfort you.
　　Take it, be mistress, be wife of it all."

　　She nothing answers, remembering winter nights
　　and the nails' snap, and the shingles' wearing chatter
　　and the pitted ruin of the last woodpecker's clatter.

　　"You have seen me at harvest, you know I can pitch my share.
　　I am strong as my father was, and will be for many a year,
　　No weakness there."

　　She nothing answers, seeing the winnowing years
　　and the broken shell his father is, and the shell
　　his grandfather is, winnowed out by the niggling fears,
　　dry chaff, blown out, drifting out on the years.

Hollow in the wheat and blackbirds

1

Hear the black fellow in the willows,
spring-crazed, turning a dusty shake
like bubbles rising through rusty water
to break.

2

A boy shot a blackbird high on a willow.
A pinch of red feathers
slowly separated on the air
and slowly
met red feathers drifting up through water.

3

Those red badges are not for nothing.
See a cluster of blackbirds
tossed twisting into the air breaking
against a lone marauding crow.

4

Go down to the water in the heat of the day.
The pungent willow hangs heavily in the air
and the blackbirds hang in the branches.

5

Treeless, but not an idle waste,
tawny and intense!
The sun breeds tiger lilies
and red-winged blackbirds.

On the river

Beautiful and remote,
contemptuous gulls describe immaculate
            embroiderings
up prairie streams.
They are not really foreign here, but only
part of the high
infrequent reaches of the sky,
aloof, inaccessible things
and, it must be, lonely.

Along the willowed bank
the blackbirds,
busy domestic denizens,
throng in the branches and with raucous cheer
announce a thoroughly vulgar world
but friendlier.

Song, returning

Above all you notice the sun.

Though, perhaps,
a cloud as big as a hand
drifts over, opens, and tosses out
a pelter of great cold rain
immediately the sun
strikes out again.

This was what we had waited for.
See how the land smiles under it
breaking out into cactus blossom, yellow and red,
reaching up scarlet lilies
and great bold golden sunflowers
turning the slow day round
sun faced.

This was missed,
to take the day like the sunflower
hour after hour
sun kissed.

Caterpillar

This yellow velvet visitor
is a mysterious stranger
to the little boy on the street
who squats watching it ripple over concrete.

To me,
it is a deep cut bank
grown rank with willows
pungent in the blazing noons
which flowered at the appropriate time
into brilliant identical caterpillars.

The little urchin
taken to just such a place
would recall a heaven of cars on the street
rain in the gutters
fruit stores and movies and the debris
of careless living gathered behind garages, maybe.

It is the same longing for home that stirs us all.
But home is just where the child first played
as a child.
The real longing is for the irrecoverable
barely-forgotten child's world.

Waste

The patch that was waste
being too wet to plough at the ploughing
has grown to an atoll of blue in a willow reef
breeding life in an ocean of wheat.

Ducks launch their broods from the grassy margins.
Muskrats thrive in the channeled shore.
A jumping deer incredibly traces
gracefully wide-spaced, clustered patterns
Ariel to the coyote's earthbound spoor.

And the genius of the place,
the ancient, bright, sun lover, the blackbird,
rides on his blood-touched plumage through the blaze
breaking into his rich barbaric clamour of praise.

Endpiece: Burning the leaves

After the spring's benign explosion
crashing the eye with leaves, flowers,
small white parachutes of seeds drifting —

this aromatic smoke lifting,
voices of children fat with pleasure tasted,
thin grey ash.

Turnstone Press
Rock Painter by R.E. Rashley
Poetry Series Two
Number Three

Rock Painter was printed offset in an edition of 750 copies, six hundred of which are paperbound, the remaining one hundred and fifty hardbound. It is set in 10 point Theme on Classic Laid Avon paper, and was printed in July, 1978 by Charles Michalski in Winnipeg. G.E. Plosz took the cover photograph, the book was designed by Eva Fritsch.

Turnstone Press gratefully acknowledges a grant from the Canada Council which has aided in the publication of this book.

We would also like to thank The Saskatchewan Museum of Natural History for permission to reproduce the petroglyph that appears on the front cover.

Turnstone Press
St. John's College
Winnipeg, Manitoba
R3T 2M5